Guide

W9-BQD-244

Panama Canal

EDICIONES
BALBOA

CONTENTS

HISTORY

AROUND THREE MILLION YEARS AGO the waters of the Atlantic Ocean and the Pacific Ocean still merged and the South American continent was separate.

Important geological phenomena led to what is today the eastern part of the Isthmus of Panama emerging from the sea bed to form a long narrow strip of land that separated the two oceans and created a land bridge between North America and South America.

After an arduous journey across the inhospitable Darién region of the Isthmus of Panama, Vasco Nuñez de Balboa discovered in 1513 the Southern Sea, which later became known as the Pacific, thereby marking the start of the countdown for what would be the Panama Canal.

Pedrarias Dávila, the governor who founded the city of Panama in 1514 on the recently discovered Pacific coast, was charged by the Spanish crown with the mission of finding a natural site to unite the two seas. On failing to locate one, he had the Camino Real built across land. For years it was used to transport

Works in the Culebra Cut in May 1911, and a 'mule' or electric towing vehicle in the Gatún Locks in 1913.

riches and merchandise from Peru and other regions of the Pacific Coast to the famous Portobelo fairs in the Caribbean.

In 1527 the River Chagres took on a leading role that made it the decisive factor in the building of today's Panama Canal. In that

year, two Spanish sailors, Hernando de la Serna and Pablo Corzo, explored the mighty Chagres River, finding it to be navigable for fifty kilometers upriver of its mouth. It was then that the city of Cruces, a river port on the Chagres River, was founded. The Camino de Cruces road, which is partly paved, was also built, running for thirty kilometers to Panama City. Together with the Camino Real, it became the most important trade route on the American continent.

FROM CHARLES V TO THE FRENCH CANAL

Aware of the strategic and economic importance that made it possible to unite both seas, in 1534 Emperor Charles V issued a royal warrant commanding the Governor of Panama in these terms, *'having been informed that the Chagres River, which flows into the Northern Sea, can be navigated with caravels for four or five leagues, and another three or*

*four in boats, and that from there to the
Southern Sea it may be four leagues overland...
go and see that land from the Chagres River to
the Southern Sea and see how that land could
be opened up so that the Southern Sea can be
linked to the river, so that it is navigable and
what difficulties there are due to the ebbing of
the sea and the height of the land and what it
costs in monetary terms and how many men are
needed and how long it will take...'.*

The concern to join the two oceans was an
ever-present concern of the Spanish Crown,
to such an extent that orders were given to
seek other routes apart from the Isthmus of
Panama, as when in 1779 Carlos III sent
Spanish engineers to explore a route across
Lake Nicaragua.

In the nineteenth century Spain's interest
spread to other countries such as France,
England, the USA and Colombia. Geogra-
phers and explorers proposed different
routes. The German Alexander von Hum-
boldt, for example, traced on a map as many
as nine possible routes to join the Atlantic to
the Pacific.

Besides all those projects, some realistic
and many fanciful, a legal battle got underway
to control the as yet hypothetical future route.
In 1835, Colombia (the Isthmus was part of
that country) awarded building rights for an
interoceanic canal to the adventurer Charles
de Thierry, and later to several other people.
Meanwhile, in 1846, the United States and
Colombia signed an international treaty on
safe passage along the Isthmus, and the
United States and the United Kingdom agreed
on another in 1850, guaranteeing the neutrality of any canal that might be built in Central
America.

While a definitive solution was sought for
the future canal, Colombia granted North
American entrepreneurs a concession to start
up a railway across the Isthmus. Work got
underway in the city of Colón in 1852 and
finished in Panama in 1855.

Concessions to private individuals gave
way to concessions to States, several treaties
being signed between the United States and
Colombia, such as the Sullivan-Samper in 1869
and the Arosemena-Sánchez-Hulburt in 1870,
which the North American Senate rejected.

Given the lack of success of such treaties, in 1878 the Colombian Congress approved the Salgar-Wise Agreement, which granted to a French company a 99-year concession for the building and operation of a canal on the Isthmus of Panama. That concession was the legal basis for the construction of what came to be known as the French Canal.

THE FRENCH CANAL

With the inauguration of the Suez Canal in 1869, Ferdinand de Lesseps, its builder, became a universally well-known figure. It was he who decided, at a Congress held by the Paris Geographical Society on 15 May 1879, where the Panama Canal should be built.

On 1 January 1880, the first symbolic shovelful of earth of this enormous project was dug at the mouth of the Rio Grande on Panama's Pacific coast. Work did not get seriously underway, however, until two years later. In 1884 over 17,000 workmen, mostly from the Caribbean islands, laboured to dig a huge trench.

The project was so ambitious, involved so many French engineers and technicians, such

From left to right, a French excavator at the foot of Cerro del Oro in 1896; reconstruction works on the Madden Dam in 1933, and the SS Ancón crossing the Culebra Cut on 15 August 1914, the day that the Canal was officially opened. Below, a founding member certificate from the French company.

as Gustave Eiffel, the designer of the tower that bears his name in Paris, and the fame of Ferdinand Lesseps was so great that thousands of French people bought shares in the *Compagnie Universelle du Canal Interoceanique* in order to help finance the works. The successful construction of the Suez Canal was a guarantee for those thousands of small investors.

But the tropics are not the same as the dry, almost desert, climate of the Suez Canal. Panama's tropical jungles protect a very fragile soil, which when the green mantle protecting it disappears and it is lashed by abundant and prolonged rainfall, quickly crumbles away. In a few hours the heavy rains destroyed the work of entire weeks, even months, making deadlines longer and budgets higher and taking the company to bankruptcy. Its many outraged shareholders accused the project managers of corruption. In 1890 there were scarcely one thousand workers still in their jobs.

In 1894 the *Compagnie Nouvelle* was set up in a final attempt by the French to rebuild the Canal, but it was to no avail. Besides the lack of financial resources, diseases, such as

malaria and yellow fever, decimated the working population. In 1903 there were barely 700 workers left.

From 1882 to 1903 the French removed over sixty million cubic meters of earth, built many bridges, railway lines, ports and hospitals and made navigation channels at both entrances to the Canal. Unfortunately, over 6,300 graves of technicians and workers were dug in that period.

PANAMANIAN INDEPENDENCE AND THE AMERICAN CANAL

Aware of the importance of that interoceanic maritime route and of the bad results of French efforts, the United States insisted on opening up a road, even returning to the idea of doing so via Nicaragua. However, pressure from French shareholders, represented by Philippe Bunau-Varilla, and Wall Street lawyer Nelson Cromwell, convinced President Theodore Roosevelt to opt for the Panamanian route.

Given Colombia's refusal to ratify the Herrán-Hay Treaty between the two countries, political pressure assuredly driven by strong economic pressure from the United States, hastened Panama's independence, which separated it from Colombia on 3 November 1903. Barely two weeks later, on 18 November 1903 the Isthmian Canal Convention was drawn up, also known as the Hay-Bunau-Varilla Treaty, between the new country and the United States. It granted a strip of land ten miles wide from one ocean to the other, a few parts of the capital city, certain islands in the Bay of Panama and the building, managing and protection of an interoceanic canal to the USA.

In 1904 an Isthmian Canal Commission was set up, presided over by John G. Walker, and George W. Dawis was named governor of the Central Panama Canal Zone, while William Gorgas, Chief of Health, undertook health care measures to control malaria and eradicate yellow fever.

By 1906 the plans to make the Canal based on several sets of locks were ready, and work began immediately. Lake Gatún was created artificially. Closing off the Chagres River near its mouth, the walls of the Culebra Cut were lowered, the approach culverts dredged, settlements were built, large military bases constructed to defend them and everything made ready for the inauguration of the Canal on 15 August 1914 with the passage of the freighter ANCON, the first vessel officially to cross the interoceanic Canal.

But the works on the Canal went on without interruption, while an ever-growing number of ships chose that route as it reduced voyage time by many days, with the resulting financial saving. The building of the Madden Dam in 1935, which gave rise to Lake Alajuela on the upper course of the Chagres River, was particularly significant in terms of regulating water in the Canal.

THE PANAMANIAN CANAL

Panama was not very much in agreement with the Isthmian Canal Convention of 1903, and so in 1935 and 1955 some aspects

*Above, left, a group of Spanish workers
at the works in 1913.
Below, excavation work carried out
using trains in the Culebra Cut and,
above, the Miraflores Locks in 1932.*

of it were reviewed and new financial compensation specified by the United States. Tension between the two nations increased, however, giving rise to confrontation in 1964 that involved deaths and injuries, and culminating in the breaking of diplomatic relations.

That same year, thanks to mediation by the OAE (Organization of American States), the Moreno-Bunker Declaration was signed by which both countries committed themselves to start negotiations in order to sign a new treaty. However, it was General Omar Torrijos Herrera who internationalized Panama's aspirations, leading to the signing in Washington on 7 September 1977 of the Torrijos-Carter Treaty, which came into effect on 1 October 1979.

The most important feature of the treaty was that it established a transition period of twenty years for the definitive handover to Panama of the interoceanic thoroughfare and the adjoining land, an event that was completed on 31 December 1999. Since that date the Canal has belonged to the Panamanians. A neutrality treaty for times of peace and of war was signed. It was guaranteed by Panama and the United States and has been subscribed to by the most important States in the international community.

OPERATION

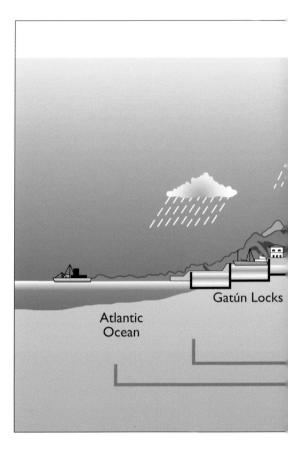

How the Panama Canal Works

THREE NATURAL FEATURES made Panama the ideal place to build an interoceanic canal: a narrow isthmus, a mighty river and exceptionally abundant rainfall. These three conditions made the engineers decide to build a canal with locks in accordance with a very simple concept in which water plays the main role.

By building a dam near the mouth of the mighty Chagres River, a navigable lake, Lake Gatún, was created about 26 meters above sea level. At one time the largest artificial lake in the world, it stores the water needed for all the lock operations.

Lake Gatún is linked to the Atlantic Ocean by a system of three-tier locks (the Gatún Locks) and an approach channel. Linking the lake to the Pacific Ocean involved crossing a small mountain range in which a trench about fourteen kilometers long was made. The Culebra Cut, as it is usually known, is also called the Gaillard Cut in memory of the engineer who carried out the project.

To reach the Pacific, two locks – the one-step Pedro Miguel and the two-tier Miraflores – were built. Both are separated by small navigable Miraflores Lake, and an approach channel links them to the ocean.

The Panama Canal operates 24 hours a day, 365 days a year. A ship coming, for example, from the Atlantic enters from Limón Bay via the approach channel along a section just over ten kilometers long as far as the Gatún Locks. This huge hydraulic lift raises the boat in three consecutive steps to Lake Gatún, situated 26 meters above sea level. A large and heavily loaded ship needs up to two hours to complete its passage through the Gatún Locks.

The ship crosses Lake Gatún along a winding course that virtually follows the original course of Chagres River, about thirty kilometers long as far as the entrance to the Culebra Cut. Recently widened so that two large-tonnage ships can cross simultaneously

Panama Canal Profile

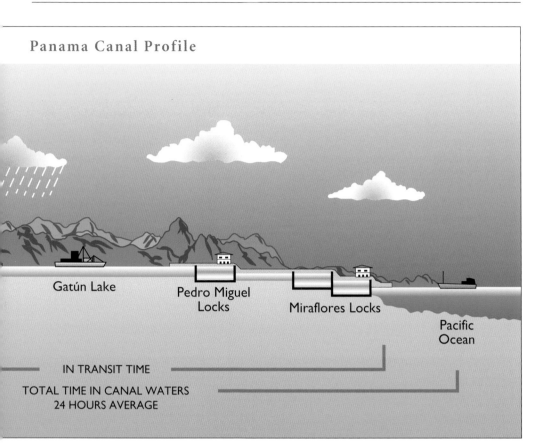

Gatún Lake

Pedro Miguel
Locks

Miraflores Locks

Pacific
Ocean

IN TRANSIT TIME

TOTAL TIME IN CANAL WATERS
24 HOURS AVERAGE

in opposite directions, it is still the narrowest part of all the navigable Canal.

The ship covers about fourteen kilometers to reach the Pedro Miguel Locks, where it drops 9.5 meters in only one step to the level of Lake Miraflores. By crossing this small lake about 1,600 meters, it reaches the Miraflores Locks, where the ship is lowered by means of the two tiers to the level of the Pacific Ocean. The ship crosses a small section of the approach channel, goes under the emblematic Bridge of the Americas and reaches the open sea.

Average total time for a ship in Canal waters ranges between 24 and 30 hours although the average transit duration through the Panama Canal is from 8 to 10 hours.

THE LOCKS

Both oceans are at the same level and the locks have the single purpose of raising the ships to the level of Lake Gatún and then lowering them in a reverse operation.

The three locks of the Panama Canal are formed by 88 sluice gates and a total of almost 250 valves that control and channel the water needed to operate the locks. They were built with technologies dating from the beginning of the twentieth century and their machinery is electrically operated.

The lock operating system is very simple. Each lock has chambers 330 meters long by 33.5 meters wide where ships move up and down using the water from the Chagres River.

Gatún Locks ■ How it works

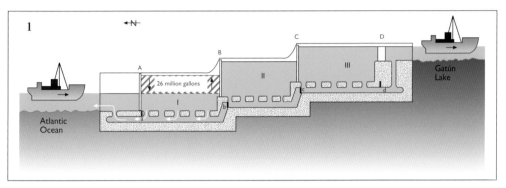

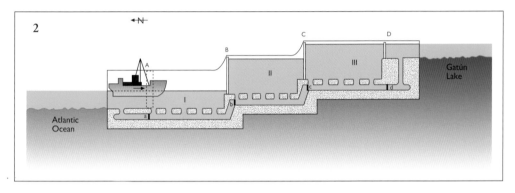

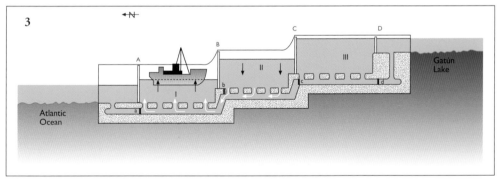

*1. As a ship transiting from the Atlantic to the Pacific approaches, the lock prepares to receive it by equalizing Chamber **I** with sea level by opening Valve **a**. In eight minutes 26 millions gallons of fresh water from Lake Gatún – where the water needed for canal operation is stored – are spilled into sea.*

*2. When the levels are the same, miter Gate **A** is opened and the ship enters Chamber **I**. Valve **a** is closed.*

*3. With this ship in Chamber **I**, miter Gate **A** is closed, and, opening Valve **b**, the ship is raised by equalizing Chambers **I** and **II**.*

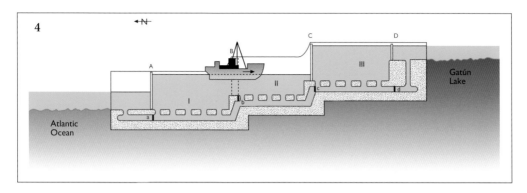

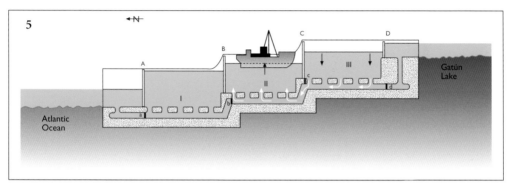

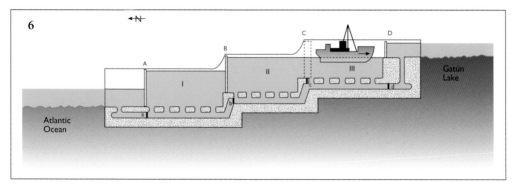

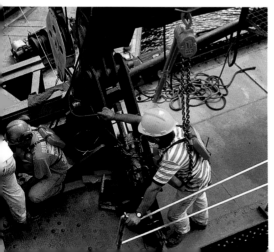

4. *After equalizing Chambers **I** and **II**, miter Gate **B** is opened and the ship moves to Chamber **II**.*

5. *Miter Gate **B** and Valve **b** are closed. Opening Valve **c**, the ship is raised by equalizing Chambers **II** y **III**.*

6. *Equalizing Chambers **II** and **III**, miter Gate **C** is opened and the ship moves into Chamber **III**.*

Left, changing locks at Gatún, a complex and highly specialized operation.

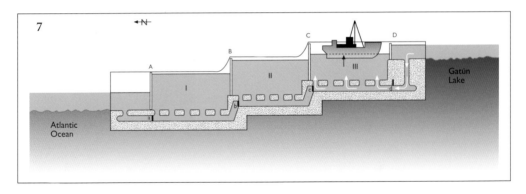

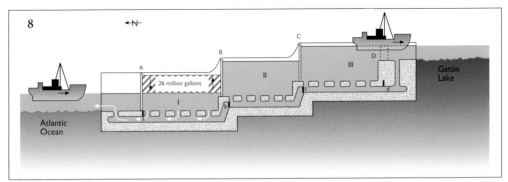

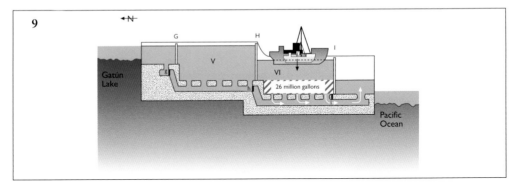

7. Miter Gate **C** and Valve **c** are closed. Opening Valve **d,** the ship is raised to the level of Gatún Lake.

8. Miter Gate **D** is opened and the ship moves into Gatún Lake, 26 meters above sea level, sailing towards the Pacific Ocean. To receive the next ship a further 26 million gallons of fresh water are released into the sea.

9. Once transit has finished on the Pacific side, the reverse process begins, by lowering the ship to sea level after releasing a further 26 million gallons of freshwater from Lake Gatún into the ocean. Except for small variations due to the tides, the amount is basically the same for every lockage whatever the size of the ship in the lock chamber.

A Panamax *going towards the Atlantic in the Pedro Miguel Locks, accompanied by mechanical towing machines. A gap of barely 60 cm separates the sides of the ship from the lock walls. Below, the Gatún control hut, which was built in 1913.*

Each lock has two sets of chambers in parallel that allow double and simultaneous lock operation. The entire process is based on the principle of communicating vessels along which the water flows by gravity, seeking the level between the chambers.

Although the system does not involve any pumps, there is a special component consisting of towing locomotives ('mules'), essential components that ensure rapid and safe transit as well as effective control of the vessels during lock operation. It is worth bearing in mind that the widest *Panamax* leaves less than sixty centimeters of space on each side of the lock walls.

The towing locomotives are used for towing, braking and keeping the ship centered in the chamber, preventing its coming into contact with the concrete walls. They provide ships with effective help, mainly the larger vessels, although the latter use their own propulsion machinery to move inside the locks. The maximum towing speed is three miles per hour. Four, six or eight locomotives are used depending on the size of the ship. The locomotives receive the ship at the entrance to the locks, aid it during lock operation, then release it at the exit at the other end.

THE DRAINAGE BASIN

Covering more than 326,000 hectares, the Panama Canal's drainage basin is without a doubt the basic tool of this interoceanic waterway. Water is the cornerstone of Panama Canal operation, and managing it is one of the basic priorities of the Canal Board.

Without the Chagres River it would not have been possible to create the Panama Canal. Between 1906 and 1913 the river was dammed, forming an artificial lake, Lake Gatún, which at a height of 26,67 meters occupies 436 km^2 and contains over 775 million m^3 of water. Lake Gatún reached a maximum height of 26,81 meters on 12 December 1993, whereas the minimum of 24.56 meters occurred on 17 May 1997.

The Madden Dam, upwater of the Chagres River, was built between 1932 and 1935, giving rise to Lake Alajuela at 76.81 meters, with a surface area of 50.2 km^2 and an active

Above, overall view of the Gatún lock system. Below, Lake Alajuela.

storage capacity of 651 million m^3 of water. Lake Alajuela reached maximum elevation of 78.60 meters on 20 December 1983, while the minimum level of 57.95 meters being was recorded on 1 August 1976.

Miraflores Dam, the smallest of the three, was built in 1914 at an elevation of 16.46 meters and with a surface area of 3.94 km^2 and water storage capacity of around 2.46 million m^3.

Co-ordinated use of the three dams makes it possible to guarantee a minimum draught of water in Lake Gatún so as to ensure uninterrupted transit of vessels. The Canal's Department of Hydrometeorology is responsible for carrying out ongoing hydrological analyses in the basin, using a complex telemetric network that provides information every fifteen minutes for 365 days of the year. It also co-ordinates the weather forecasts, flood control and analysis of lake sediment.

Its main function, however, is to ensure safe shipping for Canal users every day of the year. It ensures a minimum draught of 12.04 meters, as well as a safety zone of 1.52 meters between the Canal bottom and the ships' keels. As the Canal bottom is 11.28 meters

high, the minimum level of the lake for normal transit must be 24.84 meters. The various works to deepen the Canal bottom mean that nowadays transit through Lake Gatún does not present any problems.

Furthermore, storms and flooding are a continual threat to Canal operation in the rainy season. During those months a team of professionals is kept on alert to operate, if necessary, the spillways of the Gatún and Madden dams, or even the drains of the Gatún and Pedro Miguel locks. During this period the hydrologists need to keep a reserve or empty space in the lakes to be able to react immediately when heavy flooding occurs.

The worst storm in the Canal Basin in the last thirty years occurred on 4 and 5 Dec-

ember 1985 when the water level in Lake Gatún rose 5.1 centimeters in an hour, which
made it necessary to open the sluice gates of
Gatún Dam. On 3 and 4 November 1966, as
a result of a severe storm, the level of Lake
Alajuela rose 40 centimeters in two hours,
1.85 meters in five hours and over 2.59 meters
in twelve hours. Fortunately the level was low
and it was not necessary to open the sluice
gates of the Madden Dam.

MAINTENANCE
AND MODERNIZATION

The Panama Canal, the world's foremost
interoceanic waterway, requires continu-
ous maintenance and constant moderniza-
tion of its installations. So the locomotives or
'mules' were replaced in the first few years of
the twenty first century by powerful *Mitsub-
ishi* machines. Every year the Canal Authority
invests over two hundred million dollars in
maintenance and improvements.

The Culebra Cut has also just been widened
as it used to be a bottleneck that hampered

*Above, a cruise ship going through
the Miraflores Locks and, on the right,
the Gatún Locks.
Left, the Gatún Locks control room.*

Canal operation. Henceforth two *Panamax*-size ships will be able to transit alongside each other. The mechanical machinery, which functions with valves and sluice gates, is also being replaced by modern systems with hydraulic pistons, which besides being more effective, considerably reduce maintenance requirements. There is effective monitoring of all ships in transit via advanced satellite technology, and the Canal continues to try to keep pace and meet the demands of international trade by looking into the possible construction of a third set of locks.

Right, lower part of the control deck of Miraflores Locks, which preserves technology from the beginning of the twentieth century in perfect condition and operational.

PROTECTED AREAS
IN THE CANAL BASIN

THE LARGE AREAS OF FOREST covering the Panama Canal Basin act like a huge sponge that receives heavy precipitation in the rainy period, protecting the soils from erosion, preventing excessive sedimentation in the lakes and returning much of the retained water to the rivers.

Aware of the importance of these jungles, successive Panamanian governments have set up a network of national parks and other protected areas in the Canal Basin. The aims are to ensure that the hydraulic resources function well and host high biodiversity, with a great variety of animal and plant species, many of them in danger of extinction elsewhere on the American continent.

CHAGRES NATIONAL PARK

Created in 1985 on 129,000 hectares of land, it is located in the provinces of Pa-

Above, a guayacán *in flower. Left, aerial view of the basin of the River Chagres and, below, a harpy eagle, Panama's national bird, which occurs in stable numbers in the Canal Basin.*

nama and Colón. Its rainforests generate over 40 % of the water that the Canal uses for normal operation, and provide drinking water for Panama City and Colón, which account for 50 % of Panama's population.

Although it is true that without the Chagres River building the Panama Canal would not have been possible, it is equally true that without Chagres National Park the river would not have existed. The Chagres River was known in the colonial period as the crocodile river for the large numbers of caimans and crocodiles living there.

Its steep terrain is covered in thick primary forests containing over 1,180 species of plants, many of which are endemic. Its rich wildlife is also very noteworthy, with 638 species of wild vertebrates, including 351 birds. The Camino Real crosses this national park across the Boquerón Sector. In the upper part of Lake Alajuela, a community of Embera Indigenous people has settled.

Soberanía National Park

Created in 1980, it occupies a vertical strip of flat land with hills along the eastern bank of the Panama Canal, only twenty five kilometers from the Panamanian capital. The Chagres River crosses the national park at the village of Gamboa. Its many tributaries rise in this protected area.

Moist tropical forest and very moist premontane forest cover this land, which is home to over 1,300 species of vascular plants, 59 of them endemic. More than 700 species of vertebrates live here, with 525 species of birds, including the threatened harpy eagle.

The best known trail is the Camino del Oleoducto, which is very interesting for its birdlife. The El Charco Interpretation Trail ends at a pool of crystal clear water. It is also possible to cross a restored section of the old paved part of the famous Camino de Cruces, which was used by the Spanish in the colonial period. Alongside the park is Summit Botanical Garden.

View of the Panama Canal, whose eastern shore is protected by Soberanía National Park. Left, a scarlet macaw.

CAMINO DE CRUCES NATIONAL PARK

Covering 4,950 hectares of land parallel to the Panama Canal, it was created in 1992 between Soberanía National Park to the north and Metropolitano Nature Park to the south in order to guarantee protection of a broad swathe of the Canal's eastern bank.

Its gentle rolling terrain is carpeted in thick moist tropical forest containing rich fauna and flora that has yet to be studied in depth. It is crossed by several water courses that discharge directly into the Canal.

Its great natural wealth is complemented by the great historic and cultural value of the Camino de Cruces, with a restored stretch with typical paving stones and other open sections of the historic Spanish colonial road.

The spanish colonists used the road to transport pre-columbian gold and treasure taken from Peru, Baja California and Chile from Panama City to Portobelo.

ALTOS DE CAMPANA NATIONAL PARK

Left, Altos de Campana National Park and, below, a recreational area in Soberanía National Park. Above, remains of the former colonial road in Camino de Cruces National Park and, below, the threatened golden poison arrow frog.

This was the first national park to be created in Panama, in 1966, covering 4,925 hectares of land on the western bank of the Canal. Campana Hill, 850 meters above sea level, which contains many endemic plant, is a spectacular lookout point that affords exceptional views of the Canal Basin and Chame Bay.

Its past volcanic activity is reflected in its rugged terrain, with spectacular cliffs and lava fields. Several of the Canal basin rivers rise here. It is covered in moist forest, very moist tropical forest and rainforest, where 198 tree species and 342 species of shrub have been recorded. The many vertebrates include a wealth of amphibians – 62 species – and rep-

Preceding double page, a spectacular meander of the River Chagres in the national park of the same name. Right, the installations at the Smithsonian Institute for Tropical Research at Isla Barro Colorado Natural Monument. Below, left, a two-toed sloth and, right, an eye-catching passion flower.

tiles - 86 species. There are seven endemic species, including the outstandingly beautiful and rare, as well as diminutive, endangered golden frog.

ISLA BARRO COLORADO NATURAL MONUMENT

Between 1911 and 1914 Loma Palenquilla, on one of whose banks hosts the site known as Barro Colorado, became an artificial island when the land was flooded to form Lake Gatún. In 1923 it was declared a biological reserve, and since 1946 has been run by the Smithsonian Tropical Research Institute.

In 1979, when the Torrijos-Carter Treaty came into force, five adjacent peninsulas on dry land were added, increasing the surface area to 5,364 hectares. Its tropical forests, in the heart of the Canal Basin, are the most studied in the world. A modern visitor center and two guided trails are available for visitors to this exceptional natural laboratory.

In the Canal Basin there is another series of protected areas, such as Metropolitano Nature Park at the gates of Panama City, Lake Gatún Recreational Area and the various protected buffer forests the lake. They all aim to conserve forest biodiversity in the Canal Basin, which is the basis of the operations of this interoceanic waterway. Its operating system is based on renewable resources, with a special role accorded to the water from one river – the Chagres – the only large river in the world whose waters discharge into two different oceans: the Atlantic and the Pacific.

THE FUTURE
OF THE CANAL

O N 22 OCTOBER 2006, the people of Panama approved the expansion of the Panama Canal by means of a referendum. The country's economic future and leadership of world maritime trade were at stake.

The current lock system, dating from 1914, posed a series of limitations in the face of the growing demands of maritime traffic. The first and essential factor was the size of the lock gates, which restricts the number of crossings; bigger gates would allow ships larger than the so-called *Panamax* vessels to travel along the Canal. The second factor is that well founded estimates indicate that the Canal will reach its maximum capacity of 330 million tons between 2009 and 2012, a figure that amounts to nearly 14,000 annual high-draft crossings.

Over a five-year period more than 120 studies supervised by national and international experts analysed Panama's future economic viability. All the variables that might affect this macro-project to increase the Canal's operating capacity – environmental impacts, project funding and profitability, social repercussions and different engineering solutions – have been analysed.

The result of all the research was a proposal to set up a third set of locks, an idea that has met with the approval of the Panamanian people. In combination with

Components of the project

1. *Deepening the inlets into the Pacific and Atlantic.*

or the third set of locks

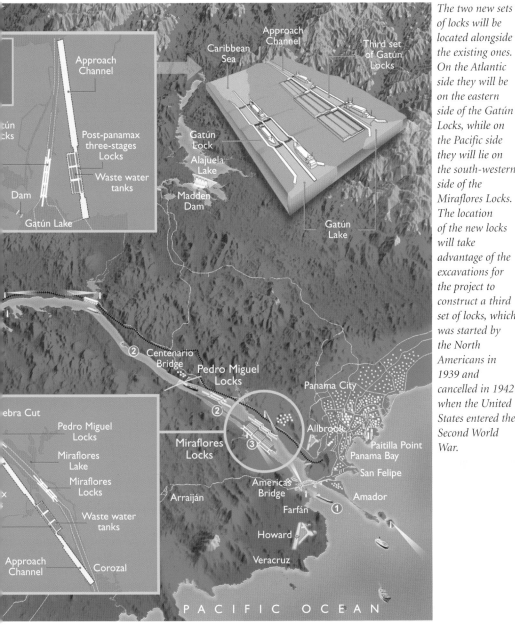

The two new sets of locks will be located alongside the existing ones. On the Atlantic side they will be on the eastern side of the Gatún Locks, while on the Pacific side they will lie on the south-western side of the Miraflores Locks. The location of the new locks will take advantage of the excavations for the project to construct a third set of locks, which was started by the North Americans in 1939 and cancelled in 1942 when the United States entered the Second World War.

Broadening and deepening [la]ke Gatún's navigation [ch]annels and increasing [th]e depth of the Culebra [(G]aillard) Cut.

3. *Building the new locks and water saving basins in the Atlantic and Pacific, complete with navigation channels.*

4. *Raising the peak operating level of Lake Gatún.*

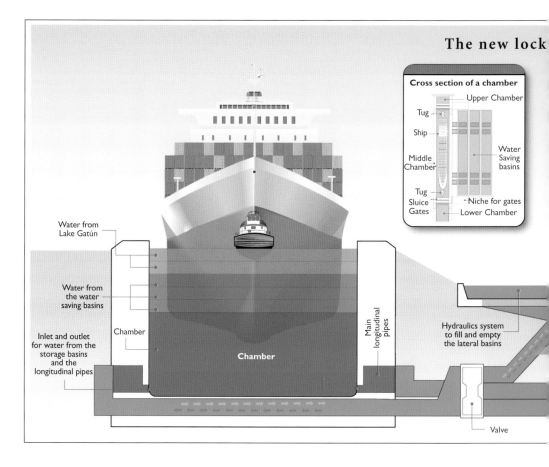

The new lock

Cross section of a chamber
- Upper Chamber
- Tug
- Ship
- Water Saving basins
- Middle Chamber
- Tug
- Sluice Gates
- Niche for gates
- Lower Chamber

Water from Lake Gatún

Water from the water saving basins

Inlet and outlet for water from the storage basins and the longitudinal pipes

Chamber

Chamber

Main longitudinal pipes

Hydraulics system to fill and empty the lateral basins

Valve

- *Ships with more than double the load of today's vessels will be able to travel through the Canal.*

- *The new locks will use less water.*

- *The locks will have rolling gates instead of the current miter gates, which will enable* in situ *maintenance to be carried out without temporary closure.*

- *Tugs will be used instead of locomotives to help the ships manoeuvre inside - a safe procedure that is used in all the world's major locks.*

Right, a container ship moving through the Miraflores Locks.

the existing locks, it would involve the passage of up to 600 million tons a year, almost double current maximum capacity. Furthermore, it will enable modern post-*Panamax* ships to use the Canal.

A PROJECT UNDERWAY

Following approval, the Panama Canal authorities initiated the project, which involves investment of over five thousand million dollars over the next eight years, with funding coming, in the main, from income generated by toll increases.

In overall terms, construction of the Third Locks involves four major actions: deepening the approach channels in the

igger and more efficient

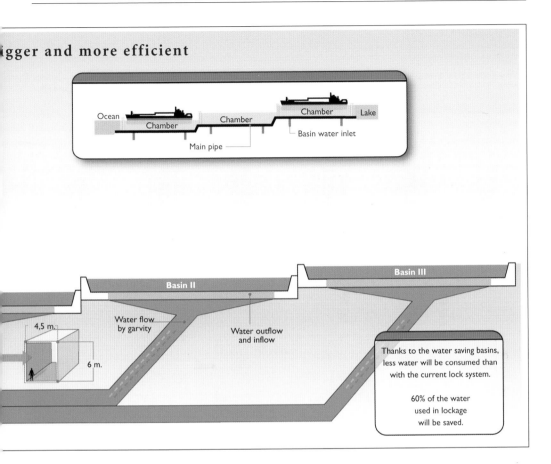

Ocean   Chamber   Chamber   Chamber   Lake

Main pipe

Basin water inlet

Basin II

Basin III

4,5 m.

6 m.

Water flow by garvity

Water outflow and inflow

Thanks to the water saving basins, less water will be consumed than with the current lock system.

60% of the water used in lockage will be saved.

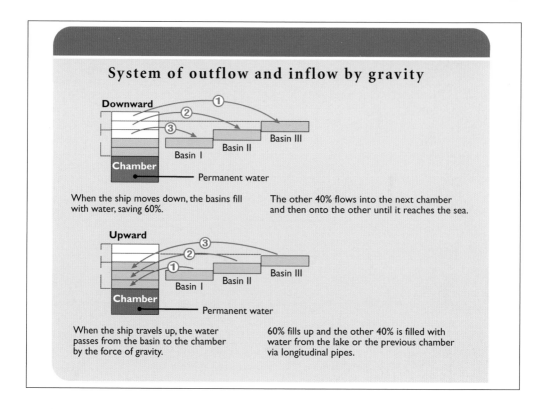

System of outflow and inflow by gravity

Downward

③ ② ①

Basin III

Basin II

Basin I

Chamber

Permanent water

When the ship moves down, the basins fill with water, saving 60%.

The other 40% flows into the next chamber and then onto the other until it reaches the sea.

Upward

③ ② ①

Basin III

Basin II

Basin I

Chamber

Permanent water

When the ship travels up, the water passes from the basin to the chamber by the force of gravity.

60% fills up and the other 40% is filled with water from the lake or the previous chamber via longitudinal pipes.

- *The new locks with their water saving basins use less water than the existing locks.*

- *The basins save 60% of water used in each lockage.*

Pacific and Atlantic; widening and deepening the navigation channels on Lake Gatún and deepening the Culebra Cut or Gaillard Cut; constructing new locks in both oceans, with the corresponding navigation channels; and raising the maximum operating level at Lake Gatún.

The Canal maintenance staff's experience in dredging and excavation operations and techniques has enabled them, with their own funds, to initiate the works on both Canal entrances in the Culebra Cut, Lake Gatún and in the approach channels. The dredging works will continue over the eight years scheduled for project completion. Lock construction is scheduled to start in 2008, and the work to raise the water level in Lake Gatún will commence in 2011.

On the Atlantic side of the Canal, the new lock will be located to the east of the current Gatún Lock, while on the Pacific

The huge Panamax vessels move through the Miraflores Locks aided by powerful mechanical mules.

side it will be housed southwest of the existing Miraflores Locks. The site of the new locks was chosen to take advantage of excavations made according to North American plans for a Third Set of Locks which began to be implemented in 1939; the project was halted in 1942 when the United States of America entered the Second World War.

The new locks, each consisting of three sections, will be larger, more efficient and more ecological. They will permit the transit of ships with more than double the load of today's vessels. The most important new features include the construction of water saving basins, which save 60% of the water used for lockage.

The lock chambers will fill and empty thanks to the force of gravity. When the ship is on its way down, the basins fill with 60% of the water from the chamber, while the other 40% flows into the next chamber or into the sea. When the ship moves up, 60% of the basins fill up the chamber by gravity and the other 40% fill with water from the lake or the previous chamber.

The new locks will have rolling gates instead of the mitre gates of the current ones. This will enable maintenance to be performed on site without temporary closure. Another new feature is that the boats will be guided into the locks by tugboats instead of locomotives or 'mules'.

Water is the basic element that is indispensable for the sound operation of the Canal. More vessel crossings will demand greater water requirements, bearing in mind that Lake Gatún's water resources are essential for the people of the two major cities and for the sound operation of the trans-Isthmus channel, in both dry and wet seasons. The projects to deepen the navigation channels and raise the maximum level of Lake Gatún will increase the lake's water storage capacity and facilitate optimum utilisation of this important natural resource.

Construction of the new locks will enable Panama to continue as the hub of international maritime trade. Between 2007 and 2014 construction will lead to the creation of over 40,000 direct and indirect jobs. About 7,000 people will be directly involved in the building work. This will boost the country's economy, exports will grow, gross national product will rise and tourism will increase. Thanks to this huge engineering project, Panama's future will be guaranteed.

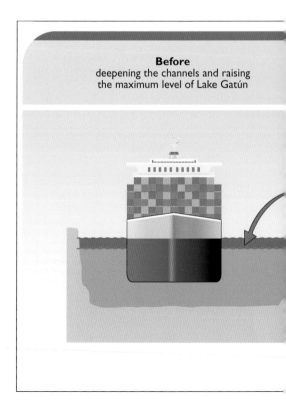

Before
deepening the channels and raising the maximum level of Lake Gatún

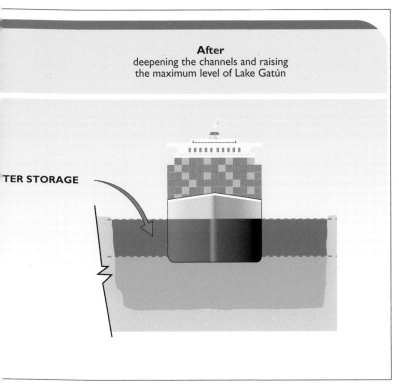

After
deepening the channels and raising
the maximum level of Lake Gatún

TER STORAGE

This vessel from the Caribbean passes through the Gatún Locks on its way to the Pacific.

The plans for the water supply consist in deepening the navigation channels and raising the peak level of Lake Gatún. These two projects will increase Lake Gatún's storage capacity and ensure the water supply both for the population and for Canal operation.